Welford

The Legacy

Welford

The Legacy

1856 to 1980

Compiled by
Barry Crowther

Published by
Matador
12 Manor Walk, Coventry Road
Market Harborough
Leics LE16 9BP, UK
Tel: (+44) 1858 468828 / 469898
Fax: (+44) 1858 431649
Email: books@troubador.co.uk
Web: www.troubador.co.uk/matador

ISBN 1 899293 62 0

Cover: View of West End, reproduced from a hand-coloured postcard commissioned by Arthur Goodfellow in 1912.

Typesetting: Troubador Publishing Ltd, Market Harborough, UK
Printed and bound by H Charlesworth & Co Ltd, Huddersfield, UK

Matador is an imprint of Troubador Publishing Ltd

Contents

Introduction

This is a pictorial history of the village of Welford, some of its people and events spanning the period 1856 to 1980. From the middle of the 19th Century, amateur and professional photographers have been recording life in our towns and villages, leaving Welford in particular with a wealth of pictures. This book reprints a selection from the many hundreds of photographs and postcards featuring local scenes.

Many of the photographs have never been published before, and the selection is biased towards the 20th Century to allow a wide range of subjects to be covered.

There are ten chapters in the book, each covering different aspects of local life. Chapter 1, 'Gateways to Welford', focuses on the three approaches to the village. The photographs and postcards, produced between 1904 and 1974, are arranged to form an anti-clockwise tour of Welford, starting at the southern end.

Next, 'Inns and Pubs' covers seven of the inns in existence during the period the book covers, plus the Cross Keys, which was de-licensed before 1847. Highlights of this section include the three inns owned by Phipps & Co in the first part of the 20th Century, the Crown, the Wheat Sheaf and the Peacock, all photographed on the 12th March 1903. The pictures are from the Phipps collection of public house photographs housed at the Northampton Museums and Art Gallery.

The most outstanding pictures in Chapter 3, 'Church, Chapel and School', are the two very early photographs of St Mary's Church, taken in 1855 or 1856 by pioneering photographer the Rev. William Law.

There were once numerous shops in the village, and most are included in Chapter 4, 'Open all Hours'. A charming photograph of George William Bird – standing in front of his grocery shop in 1922 – is of particular interest. Chapter 5, 'On the Move', features various forms of transport in and around the village before the use of the motor car became widespread.

The core of the book is devoted to people. Chapter 6, 'Work and Play', looks at some of the business folk and tradesmen, carnivals and fetes, clubs, institutions and societies in Welford. There was, and still is, a wealth of talent in this Northamptonshire village.

Fine architecture is the theme of Chapter 7, 'Rural Retreats', with Sulby Hall featuring prominently. This chapter also includes a previously unpublished photograph from the early 1930s of the Queen Mother when she was Duchess of York, with Princess Elizabeth, our present Queen.

Many changes occurred in the village after 1967, when Wakefield Drive was built, and through the 1970s, when many buildings were demolished. Chapter 8, 'The Changing Village', sets out to illustrate this. Most of the photographs in this chapter were taken by Geoff Pitcher, who faithfully recorded each event as it happened.

Chapter 9, 'Waterways', features the reservoir, River Avon and canal. The outstanding photograph in this chapter is of Mary Gilbert with daughters Gwen and Julia on her narrowboat the Gwen Mary in 1907.

Finally, 'Welford in Colour' is devoted to 12 hand-coloured postcards, all commissioned by Arthur Goodfellow, postmaster and stationer, between 1904 and around 1920.

The seeds for this book were sown in 1999/2000, when Peter Harrison produced the *Greatest Show on Earth* as a Millennium project. This was closely followed by publication of the book *Welford, Portrait of a Northamptonshire Village* by John Dunn and his Appraisal Steering Group. Without the tremendous amount of research carried out for both of these productions, this book probably would not have happened.

The knowledge and satisfaction gained in compiling *Welford – The Legacy* have been very fulfilling. One thing is certain: Welford has been, is today and, one hopes, always will be, a happy and friendly place to live.

Barry Crowther
August 2001

Acknowledgements

Books of this nature are impossible to produce without the help of a great many people, and this one is no exception. I am very grateful to the many people who came forward with old postcards and photographs. The number has been truly staggering. Their names are listed below – apologies are offered in advance for any inadvertent omissions.

As mentioned in the Introduction to the book, John Dunn and his Appraisal Steering Group saved me endless hours of research, and I thank them for allowing me to use passages from their book as a source for many of the captions in this book.

I would also like to mention Geoff Pitcher and the late Joy Bevin; their very informative local history columns published in the *Welford Bugle* in 1975 and 1976 have proved to be a great source of information, and much has been gleaned from them, for which I am very grateful.

A number of photographs have been reproduced by permission of Northamptonshire Libraries and Information Service, and also the Northampton Museums & Art Galleries. I thank both for allowing use of those important items for the book.

Finally, I would like to give a special mention to Dennis Edensor for applying his professional expertise to all the captions in the book. Without his help and guidance, the final product would not have been so interesting or informative.

Marjorie Allen * Brian Barber * Stephen Barker * Joan Beeson * Charles Bevin
Lady Boardman * Audrey Bott * Mick & Fay Brooks * Sue & Trevor Burberry
Valerie Cave * Arthur & Judy Corlett * Sue & Tony Cutt * John Deacon * Anne &
John Dunn * Dennis Edensor * Fred Farnden * Bill & Dorothy Gardner * Betty
Goodfellow * Lester Goodman * Peter Harrison * John Haynes * Sheila Hollis
Mrs Heard * Roger Keight * Kath & David Leebrook * Francis Lincoln * Geoff
& Vera McAlister * Terry Pettitt * Mr & Mrs Pilmore * Geoff Pitcher * Ian &
Sylvia Sandercock * Mrs Seaton * Doug & Liz Seward * Rod & Liz Scribbins
Eileen Smith * Dick Smith * Jean Tyrrell * David Vaughan * Peggy Walker

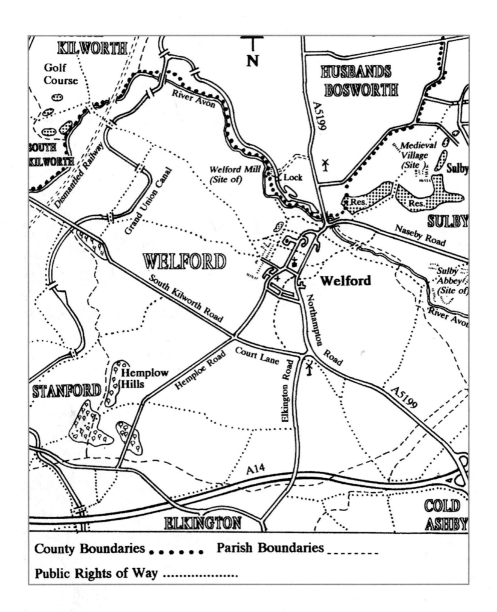

County Boundaries ●●●●●● **Parish Boundaries** - - - - - - -

Public Rights of Way ·················

1 Gateways to Welford

Toll-House Corner late 1950s. The junction of the former Northampton and Lutterworth turnpikes, just south of Welford, where tolls were collected until the 1890s. The main road, originally named the Portway, later became the A50.

Tollgate House late 1950s. Built for the toll collector, it was badly damaged by a lorry and was finally demolished in 1961. Also at the junction stood a milestone indicating 80 miles to London.

New Road, Tollgate Corner early 1960s. Improvements to ease the curve and make the junction safer resulted in the lay-by, still in use. The road today is the A5199.

Newlands Road junction 1945. The houses were built in 1932 by Brixworth Rural District Council. Some are still occupied by descendants of the original tenants. The keep-left island was removed in 1948.

Northampton Road late 1950s. The police house was built as a sub-station in 1949. An extension was added over the flat-roofed office in 1961. TV aerials were becoming increasingly common.

Welford Garage late 1950s. Owner Gus Hines also had a business in Church Lane, the left turning between Prospect House and the Reading Room. The sign heralds the Peacock Inn, also in Church Lane. The pub closed within two years of this picture.

Northampton Road 1905. Looking south towards Northampton, with the Vicarage wall on the left. Only the odd bicycle or horse and cart would have disturbed this rural scene. The building on the right is where the village garage now stands.

Snowy morning in Northampton Road in 1904. To the left is the wheelwright's business run by the Partridge family, and on the right a farm worker is at work near the Doctor's Barn. This was so called because a large slate slab used as a gate post was inscribed 'O 1828' after the village doctor J.Orton.

High Street by Church Lane 1905. The Reading Room on the left was built in 1870 for villagers to improve their education. It was used by the Home Guard in the Second World War. Later it became a shop before being converted into a private dwelling.

High Street by the former Talbot Inn 1905. The section of the Talbot on the left was demolished in 1959. On the right, the mid-18th Century chequered brick wall with high ashlar coping flanks the garden of the Manor House.

By Porter's in 1905. A delightful scene in High Street. The elegant lady with the bicycle is probably Mrs Porter with her daughter. Cycling in such a voluminous skirt must have been a liability but a more practical outfit would have been frowned upon in Edwardian times.

By Goodfellow's shop in 1904. Looking north down High Street, the shop is on the right. Children were safe playing in the road as the occasional horse and cart was the only traffic hazard.

Lower High Street 1915. The houses on the left with walled gardens were built in 1849 and have changed little externally since.

Front Street late 1950s. This was the more common name for High Street and it is still occasionally called Front Street today. The boundary wall to the houses has been rebuilt and lowered. Today, the entrance to Avon Fields is to the right of the road.

Junction with West Street 1906. The thatched cottages on the left were built around 1750–60 and survived until 1975 when they were demolished.

Leicester Road around 1910. The bridge over the River Avon was built in 1817 and the centre of it marks the boundary between Leicestershire and Northamptonshire. Note the Gilbert trading sign on the George.

From the Naseby turn 1910. This was the usual route for the many villagers who used the railway station at North Kilworth some three miles away.

From the Naseby Road 1910. This part of Welford has changed dramatically. Almost all of the buildings were demolished in the 1940s to 1960s. The row of cottages middle left is thought to be the Welford workhouse, which closed in 1834. West Street is visible upper right. The cottages were knocked down in the mid-1970s.

Naseby Turn on the A50 February 1965. The gap in the railings middle right is the old ford over the Avon, sometimes known as the Greeny Brook.
(*Reproduced by permission of Northampton Libraries and Information Service*).

From the Naseby Turn, the A50 looking south, February 1965.
(*Reproduced by permission of Northampton Libraries and Information Service*).

North entrance to Welford 1908. Bertha Copson's cottage is on the right. The Birmingham evening newspapers, which arrived at Welford and Kilworth station, were dropped off here by Mr. Adnitt, who ran a cab service.

The Square. Above, a Hillman Minx and Commer van stand at the roadside in February 1965. Below, the bus stop is where the Swan Inn later had its car park. (*Both pictures reproduced by permission of Northampton Libraries and Information Service*).

West Street by The Square 1974. It was originally Grange Street, then in 1718 it was known as Back Street. The Sulby Rise development has just been started on the right-hand side.

West Street 1930s. The water pump past the row of houses on the left was one of 73 pumps and wells in the village and among the last to be shut off. Tyrrell's Model T Ford van is just coming into view.

West Street 1905. In the distance on the left, scaffolding stands around the village hall which is just being built.

By the village hall around 1910. The tree where the boys are standing is at the front of Vine Cottage. Engine Cottage is to be seen just forward of the girls on the right. Notice the corrugated metal roof.

West Street by the school early 1950s. The above photo, looking north, shows the village hall. Below is the view south. The Manor House wall is on the left.

West End by Welford House 1905. West End retains much of its village charm nearly 100 years later.

By Oak Cottage 1960s. This is a particularly fine timber-framed building dating from around the late 17th Century.

Towards West End Farm 1910. The farmhouse in the centre of the scene was built in 1848 and has changed little externally since.

West End 1915. Visible in the middle of the fence on the right is the post box, put up in the reign of Edward VII, 1901–1910. Just visible on the right at this end of the spiked wooden fence is a water pump. A replica of this stands there today.

West End 1907 looking south from Newlands Road Corner. This area was called Overtownsend in the late 1660s. Seven of the properties once belonged to Mrs Ellen Bowen-Davies, who died in 1963 aged 89. Her land-owning father George Gee had No 7, named Oaklands, substantially renovated and gave it to her when she married. Her staff occupied No 9, first cottage on the right, which was connected to Oaklands by two hand gates.

Newlands Road around 1945. The road was made in 1778 and originally called Bakehouse Lane Road, later shortened to Bakehouse Lane. The houses in the photographs were built in 1928 by Brixworth Rural District Council.

2 Inns and Pubs

The George 1906. Mrs Gilbert with her daughters Gwen and Julia plus members of the staff. The castellations on the tower and porch were added in the mid-1800s.

1908. This is the earliest photograph of the George showing the Gilbert sign. Mrs Gilbert sold coal and other commodities which arrived by canal boat at the wharf behind the building.

The George 1904. The heavily laden cart is standing on the weighing machine installed at the inn.

1947. Mr. George Peabody's fine Armstrong Siddeley parked at the front of the George. Around this time the inn's name was changed to the Wharf.

The George Inn was built in 1814 by William Dobson. The photograph above was taken in 1897 and is the earliest of the inn to come to light. The smoke rising to the left is from the lime kilns. Old Burditt and Harry Adnitt pose with Blossom the horse. The family group is William Gilbert, his wife Mary, who is holding week-old Gwen, and Mrs. Bill Page. The name of the maid is unknown. Mr. Gilbert took the licence in 1891. On his death in 1904 it was transferred to Mrs Gilbert, who held it until 1946. Mary Gilbert is pictured left in 1888, aged 19. On the right is William Gilbert the same year.

The Swan Inn, also called the Hind, at the bottom of High Street. It was built around 1800 and these pictures were taken about 1907. The cottages on the right were demolished in the 1940s, leaving space for a car park.

The Swan was bought by Marston, Thompson and Evershed of Burton upon Trent before 1903. This is the first photograph showing the sign of Marston's Burton Ales painted on the wall.

The Swan around 1959. This is the first picture revealing Marlow Cottage, the white painted cob building behind the pub. It was previously hidden by the cottages where the car park now is.

The Crown Inn dates from the mid-18th Century. It was bought by Phipps in 1904 and closed in 1918 when the licence would not be renewed due to the number of other pubs in Welford. The above photo, taken on 12th March 1903, is held at the Northampton Museums and Art Gallery. The picture below was taken around 1907. After Phipps took over, the old sign was replaced by one which no longer mentions accommodation.

Crown Inn around 1907. Some of the children in this charming scene became the parents and grandparents of some of today's villagers. The horse and cart probably belonged to Mrs Gilbert of the George and is perhaps delivering coal. This and the cycle propped against the wall are probably the only traffic that morning.

Wheat Sheaf Inn. The picture, taken on 12th March 1903, is from the Phipps collection of public house photographs at Northampton Museums and Art Gallery. The inn's first licence was taken out in 1799.

The Wheat Sheaf 1907. It closed as a pub in February 1914. It was also used as a parcels receiving office by the London & North Western Railway. The steep kerb on the west side of High Street makes a handy resting place for children.

Shoulder of Mutton 1906. Landlady's daughter Sarah Toseland is standing at the door of the pub on the left of High Street. On the opposite side of the road is the Wheat Sheaf and the blacksmith's.

1912. Little has changed at the Shoulder of Mutton since the previous picture. The wall in the right foreground belongs to the Talbot Inn, where stagecoaches turned in until around 1850.

Shoulder of Mutton about 1910. Mrs Jane Toseland with her daughter Sarah outside the inn, built in the late 18th Century. Jane took the licence in 1901 on the death of her husband Arthur.

Busy scene outside the Shoulder of Mutton around 1907. Sarah Toseland's blouse, full-length skirt and hairstyle are typical of the period. Sarah took the licence when her mother died in 1916 and remained licensee until 1956.

The old cart entry at the Shoulder of Mutton was blocked up in 1973. By this time a new entrance door has already been built and the pub has a more modern look. The buildings to the left of the inn have been demolished for a car park.

Outside the former Talbot Inn in 1906. The largest and most famous of Welford's inns closed in 1870, but not before winning its place in the history of coaching and being immortalised by Charles Dickens in *Bleak House*.

The Talbot Inn as it looked in 1959 just before part of it was demolished. It was owned and run by Ann Spencer, right, until her retirement in 1852. In a directory of 1840 Mrs. Spencer was listed as a farmer, innkeeper and postmistress.

The Peacock Inn opened as an ale house in 1745 and was bought by Richard Phipps in 1865. It was closed by Phipps and Co in 1962, and demolished in 1973. The photo above, showing the inn on 12th March 1903, is from Northampton Museums and Art Gallery. By 1908 (below), a new sign had been erected over the door.

The former Cross Keys, on the corner of Newlands Road and West End. It was licensed from 1795 until around 1847. The building was altered in the 1960s.

3 Church, Chapel and School

Looking north down West End towards the Church in 1910. The three-storey home on the corner of Hall Lane is named Ivydene. Today the entrance to the recreation ground is on the opposite side of the road.

West End in the 1930s. The war memorial has been erected in the churchyard to honour the dead of 1914–19.

Church view around 1947. The churchyard's wooden gates can be seen, the former iron gates having been removed during the Second World War.

The church around 1922. The date can be fixed by the pristine condition of the newly erected war memorial.

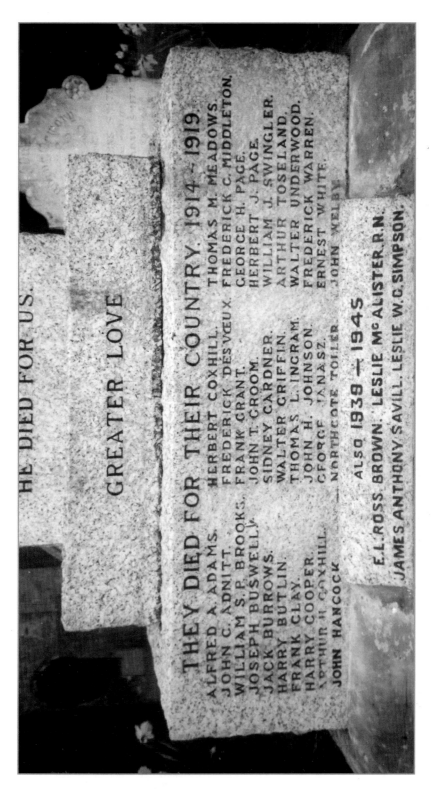

The war memorial commemorates the 30 men of the parish who fell in the First World War and four who died in the Second World War.

These two photographs are the earliest ones of St. Mary's Church. They were taken in 1855 or 1856 by Rev. William Law, Rector of Marston Trussell 1842–1900. They reveal many of the original features of the 13th Century building. The tower is 15th Century.

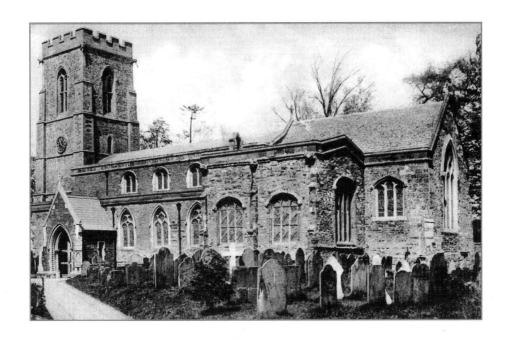

The Church in 1905. It was restored in 1872 and the north aisle rebuilt. Comparison with the photographs opposite shows the east window is much higher, the south window of the sanctuary is much shorter (it is bricked up in the earlier picture). The chancel originally had a much lower roof. The porch was rebuilt in 1872. The tracery and moulding of the windows of the south aisle were altered during the restoration and the stained glass in the tower window replaced.

The church interior when oil lamps still provided light before electricity was installed. The photograph above was taken in 1904, the one below in 1915. Note the pulpit is on the right. It was probably moved to the left side in 1918 when the crucifix to the memory of Lieutenant T. F. H. Torney was presented.

December 1953. The Sedilia (priests' seat) and opening for the Piscina (stone bowl) are discovered during work on the church.

The sanctuary in 1954.

Dedication of the sanctuary 28th May 1955. From left, Bishop of Peterborough Dr Spencer-Leeson; Archdeacon of Northampton; Rev Francis Cyprian Woodhouse, vicar 1914–1946; Rev Edward Guy Elcock, vicar 1946–1957.

The Congregational Chapel. The 1907 photograph above shows the Sunday school, which was built in 1866 at a cost of £400. Below, this picture from the late 1950s show the chapel, built in 1793, and the Manse House.

Aerial view of the school in the early 1950s. The main building was erected in 1859. The earth closets at the end of the playground were not modernised until 1951.

The school in
the 1950s.

Although not illus-
trated in this photo-
graph, the play-
ground was divided
by a railing to
segregate boys
and girls.

Only after Wakefield
Drive was built
and the Leys started
in 1970 was
the school signifi-
cantly changed
to accommodate
increasing numbers.

View of the school from School House garden.

The School House in 1952. It ceased to be used as the headteacher's home in 1978.

The earliest school photograph, taken in 1900. It is thought that the man on the left is Mr W. J. Moore, the headmaster.

School class A in 1926. Standing in the back row far left is the teacher Miss Croft. Many of the pupils will be easily recognised, they are parents and grandparents of many living in the village today.

School photograph early 1960s. It was taken on the cricket field bank in front of the Manse House.

Cast of the school Christmas pantomime December 1950.

School trip to London 1956. Bill Gardner, Ida and George Twemlow and Rev Edward Elcock.

School staff in 1951.
Mr A. Barnes, left and George Twemlow. Ida Twemlow, left and Miss D. Pike.

School staff around 1960. George and Ida Twenlow, Mrs Dorothy Gardner and Mrs Marjorie Allen.

School staff in 1974 when the new hall and canteen were added. Rear from left, Mrs Beryl Copson, Wenna Hemming, Mrs Janet Mills. Front, Mrs Helen Woolley, Ida and George Twemlow, Mrs Allen and Miss Denise Plevin.

4 Open all Hours

Tyrrell's Shop 1930 after a refit. The outside tap there today is not visible. The cottage on the right has been rebuilt with a slate roof.

Tyrrell's 1967. The cottages between the shop and the Swan have been demolished, forming a car park by the bus stop.
(*Reproduced by permission of Northampton Libraries and Information Service.*)

High Street 1906. A small shop can be seen halfway down on the left. The owner's name is unknown.

Martin's tea room late 1950s. The cottage on the right with Strawberry Gothic windows became a tea room while owned by Mr Martin the butcher. It was bought as a private house in 1962 by Cecil Lane. The roof of the Great Barn can be seen to the right of the cottage.

Bird's shop 1922. George William Bird at the shop he ran from 1889 to 1924 when he sold it to Frank Gardner. Mr Bird employed several assistants and groceries were delivered to seven other villages. Mr Gardner had been apprenticed in the grocery trade at Seymour Meads, a large business in Southport.

High Street 1906. Bird's shop on the left and, part hidden by the tree on the right, is Martin's butcher's shop. There was a slaughterhouse at the rear.

Bill and Dorothy Gardner in 1972. Bill is the son of Frank Gardner. On Frank's retirement in 1957 Bill and Dorothy took over the running of the shop, although Frank continued to work part time until his death in 1970.

Welford post office and Goodfellow's shop 1905. The 'Postie' outside the post office entrance is wearing the uniform that had become standard in 1870. Mr Goodfellow, also the postmaster, is standing outside his general store.

The post office, also in 1905, but looking south up High Street. This was the golden age of the postcard, with two million posted in the UK every day. Most were delivered next day, the postal service being the envy of the world at this time. This picture is from one of the many postcards commissioned by Mr Goodfellow.

The post office 1912. By now the telephone had been installed with the number Welford 1. The George V notice under the public telephone sign proves the photograph is later than 1911.

Slightly further up High Street 1914. Goodfellow's shop is devoid of advertising signs, giving a rather sombre look to the street.

Goodfellow's shop 1940s. Black Cat and Gold Flake were popular wartime cigarette brands. A vending machine stands by the post office door.

Frederick Ward, tailor, about 1900. This shop was next to the Shoulder of Mutton. Mr Ward is listed in Bennett's Business Directory 1901–02 as a tailor and grocer.

Porter and Sons, saddlers 1920s. The business is listed in Kelly's Directory as early as 1854. The hunting set probably made good use of the business during the season.

The Blacksmith's 1912. Directly to the right of where the man and lad are standing in High Street was the site of the blacksmith's shop. On the left, Mr Porter is standing in his shop doorway.

Nan Burton's drapery shop around 1900. Known as London House, it sold dresses, material, toys, games and dolls, all stored in tall glass cabinets. Later it became a hairdresser's and a café. Today it is the Elizabethan Country Pub and Restaurant.

Lovell's Cottage 1930s. It is the building with the attractive lamp on the corner and the site of Mr F. Bell's motor repair business. He tackled anything from welding and drilling to charging wireless batteries. The premises acted as a DIY centre for motorists and motorcyclists. Mr Bell also ran a taxi service. The entrance to Atterbury House is to the right where the young lad is about to cross the road.

Welford Garage 1964. By this time is was owned by Mr Vernon, who also ran a taxi service.
(*Both photographs reproduced by permission of Northampton Libraries and Information Service.*)

No 2 Church Lane. The site of Doris Pitcher's grocery store. She also sold newspapers, sweets and lemonade.

Scrimshaw's cobbler's shop on the left in Church Lane. It later became a fish and chip shop run by Mrs Worsdale. The former Peacock Inn is next door.

Miss Cutler's milliner's shop 1907. On the corner of Church Lane, West Street and West End. Miss Cutler also sold haberdashery and Turkish Delight. Two doors up in West End Mrs Branston sold ice-cream.

Hall Lane 1974. Site of the grocery shop run by Mrs Brooks, where she sold newspapers. It later became the post office. Today it is a private dwelling.

No 30 West End. This mid-18th Century building is thought to be one of the earliest village bakeries. West End was originally known as Bakehouse Lane before the name changed around 1777. During 1922–32 Mrs Rule ran a shop selling cigarettes and groceries. At some time before that it was home to Mr. Butlin, a tailor.

Dick Freeman, baker, in the 1920s with his delivery cart and young helper Randle. Mr Freeman also made pork pies and cooked villagers' Sunday dinners for a penny. People took their meat in a tin and Yorkshire pudding mix in a jug. The baker also delivered to other local villages.

Billy Mann ran a butcher's shop in West Street. A child stands by the shop door on the left. Almost opposite is Mr S Seaton's shoe repair shop. The village hall has been extended, placing this picture in the 1930s.

Towards the bottom of West Street, Miss Dexter ran a general store, seen here in 1965. (*Reproduced by permission of Northampton Libraries and Information Service.*)

Mrs. Finch, baker, 1930s. Her shop is on the right with the Hovis sign just visible. When the cottage on the left, near High Street corner caught fire, the fire brigade pumped so much water down the chimney, it flooded the road outside.

5 On the Move

The cab business. Harry Partridge is listed in the George Green & Co directories of 1909 and 1912 as a cab proprietor. This is him around 1907 outside the Partridge home in West Street with his cab and female members of the family.

Harry Partridge's immaculately turned out cab at the vicarage gate in Northampton Road around 1907.

The old stagecoach 1895. The Partridge family ran a blacksmith's and a wheelwright's business on Northampton Road on the site which became the garage. Three generations of the family are pictured: J. C Partridge is on the left, the children are Harry and sister Ella, and Jim Partridge is on the right. The coach ended its days as a garden shed.

Harry Partridge pauses in grooming one of the horses used to pull his cab. Sister Ella keeps a watchful eye in this 1907 scene.

Down at the George Inn, Old Burditt and Harry Adnitt prepare to set off delivering coal for Mrs Gilbert in 1897. The horse was called Blossom.

Little is known about this superb scene by the Manor House wall in West Street, probably around 1900. The cricket bat is typical of those used in the late 19th Century. Perhaps the pair are off to play for the village team?

1916 at Sulby Abbey Farm. Miss Francis May Jones and sister Muriel in their favourite trap that would take them on trips to Market Harborough. The sisters often joined baker Dick Freeman on his delivery round.

The Watney Red Rover stagecoach and four crossing the bridge over the River Avon by the Wharf Inn around 1965 during a brewery promotional exercise.

Goodfellow's horse and cart in 1904. It made grocery deliveries around the area. A bottle of Midland Pure Malt Vinegar sold at Goodfellow's around this time was found by William Warner of Welford in 1999. He presented it to the village and it is now on display in the post office.

Busy scene at Welford and Kilworth station in the 1920s. Bales of wool are being unloaded from the cart ready for transit by train.

The Miller's carrier around 1900. Return journeys to Market Harborough on Tuesday, Northampton Wednesday and Saturday. The carrier was used until around 1920 when a bus service was started. Dennis Miller at the reigns with Marcia Miller and Tom Miller on the right.

The Miller Family around 1900. Back from left: John, Annie, Thomas snr, Sally, Amos and Frederick. Middle: William, Maria, Dennis, Charles, Thomas jnr. Front: Frank and Alice.

Thomas Miller started a bus service in Welford in 1920. He used this chain-drive, converted lorry reg no. BD 4783. The body was removable so that the lorry could carry goods.

Mr Miller also ran this 14-seat American Chevrolet lightweight.

In 1931 United Counties took over Miller's bus service. Local Bobby PC Frost with bus driver in 1935. This photograph was taken outside the United Counties bus garage at the bottom of West Street.

Fred Farnden, chauffeur to Major Paget of Sulby Hall, with the Pagets' 15.9 HP Morris Oxford in Spain in the late 1920s. Fred's son, also Fred, still has the car's original 1927 manual price 1/6 (7½p). The photograph is thought to have been taken by Ann Taylor, lady's maid to Mrs Paget, with a Kodak Box Brownie camera.

Bull Nose Morris near Primrose Cottage in the early 1930s. The cottages where the car is parked were demolished in 1949.

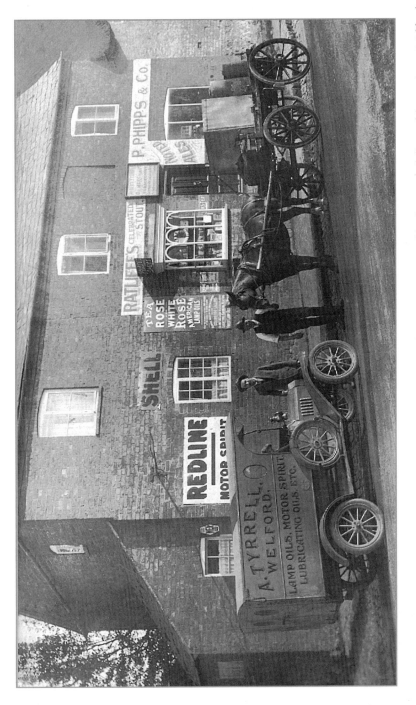

Tyrrell's Model T Ford 15cwt van 1920. Probably the first commercial motor van in Welford. It was delivered by train to Welford and Kilworth station and Roland Tyrrell, then 17, drove it to Welford despite never having driven before. The van gave years of service but the windscreen eventually became so discoloured that Mr Tyrrell had to drive looking out of the side.

The Goodfellow family's cars included this Singer Junior tourer 1927–32.

The family also owned this fine American Studebaker Erskine 1926–30. It boasted a 2.3 litre six-cylinder engine.

More frugal transport was offered by this Ford Prefect pictured April 1952.

Whit Sunday 1964. Jack and Jim Vaughan pause in West End before moving under steam to a steam engine rally at Stanford Hall. William Bevin and Robert Adkins are pictured hoping to cadge a lift.

One of the Vaughan family's three steam engines being used for threshing. All were moved under steam to the old tip in 1947 to be cut up for scrap for £10 each.

Vaughan's saw mill working here in Knight's Lane Field. The wood-framed rack bench could take felled timber up to 3ft diameter.

Field Marshal Series III single-cylinder tractor, one of two bought in 1946.

Roland Tyrrell and Excelsior motorcycle with his brother-in-law on the pillion. They are by Tyrrell's petrol pumps at the bottom of High Street.

Members of the Partridge family outside Vine Cottage in High Street in the late 1920s with a sporty motorcycle and sidecar.

Gwen Gilbert and companion on a belt-driven 499cc Triumph in the 1920s. This type of motorcycle was used by despatch drivers in the First World War and proved to be so reliable they were dubbed 'Trusties'.

Perambulator 1932 style. Jean Tyrrell, a few months old, in the High Street with gran and auntie. The pram was the latest model.

Julia Gilbert, left, and sister Gwen with their prized bikes outside the George Inn in 1909.

Harry Partridge in Church Lane. Always immaculately dressed, Harry is sporting his usual stiff collar for this pose in 1905.

Approach to Welford and Kilworth station 28th March 1916. Workmen take a break from clearing snow from the road after blizzards swept the Midlands.

The station around 1930. Opened in the 1850s, it was very important to Welford people. Many cycled the three miles to catch trains to Rugby or Market Harborough. In 1938 the station had a staff of eight.

Aerial view of Welford and Kilworth station in the late 1950s. The dairy on the opposite side of the road closed in 1964 due to a decline in rail traffic.

The view along the Market Harborough to Lutterworth Road past the station in the 1940s. The station would have been built nearer to Welford if Mrs Spencer of the Talbot Inn had been prepared to sell land to the London and North Western Railway Company in the mid-1800s.

William Stocks was the signalman for
40 years from 1896. He is seen here at
the levers before his retirement
on 10th May 1936.

The last train from
Peterborough to Rugby.

The last passenger train at
Welford and Kilworth on
4th June 1966 before the
station closed forever.

6 Work and Play

Harry Partridge on a cart around 1907. It is not known who the other men are. The likely location is a barn by the tollgate corner.

Harry Partridge again, with his dog in the garden of Welford House. He later moved to West End Farm.

Harry Partridge on 16th July 1909 stands alongside the butcher, who has probably just taken delivery of this new looking cart. John Coulson Partridge & Son are listed in Kelly's Northamptonshire Directory of 1914 as carriage builders so they may have supplied the vehicle.

Ezra Ball the blacksmith, centre, outside his High Street premises next to the old Wheat Sheaf around 1930.

Phil Coleman the chimney sweep on the right with his family. He worked from the old Wheat Sheaf and drove a car with a dicky seat and big bulbous horns. It was very popular for weddings.

Stan Pitcher, right,
painter and decorator,
in his yard behind
No 2 Church Lane.
His younger brother,
Cecil, is on the left.
This photo was taken
in the late 1930s.

Tools are being sharpened
by the grinder who toured
the village in the 1950s.
He is pictured here
outside Gardner's farm
in West End.

PC 'Bobby' Frost in 1934 at one of his
regular spots outside the church gates.

Arthur John Goodfellow, postmaster and stationer, at the age of 90 in 1958 when he was Britain's oldest sub-postmaster. He took the job in 1890 at the age of 21 and died aged 97 in 1965. His foresight, in having photographs taken of the village for post-cards every two or three years from 1904 to around 1920, ensured an accurate record of Welford's buildings remains.

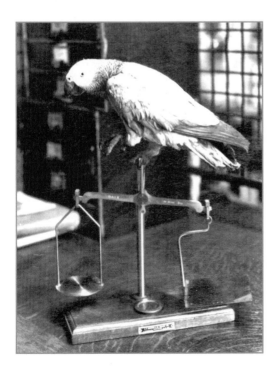

His parrot Polly Joe, also pictured in 1958, greeted customers for years. It was so named as there was doubt as to its gender.

The Gardner brothers in 1923. From left, William, George, Harry, Frank, Jack and Edgar. The gap in the the line was left in honour of brother Sidney, killed in the First World War.

Albert Freeman, pictured here in 1916, was a sergeant in the 3rd Battalion of the Grenadier Guards. Born in 1893, he died at the age of 95 in 1988. He became a captain and commanding officer of the local home guard in the Second World War.

Sergeant Freeman is pictured with Sergeant Hart, standing, in 1917.

Dad's Army. Welford Home Guard 1944.

Threshing by
Newlands Road
around 1900.

A break in
threshing in
the yard
of the Talbot
in 1910
for farmer
John Gee of
Salford House.

Also in the
Talbot yard.
John Freeman
is the yard
foreman.

Thomas and George Knight during roof repairs at Knight's Cottages in West Street in the1890s. Notice the wooden scaffolding. It hardly looks safe enough to bear a man's weight.

Maypole dancers 1905 on the ground behind the Great Barn, where Salford Close was built.

Maypole in 1908 in the grounds of Salford House.

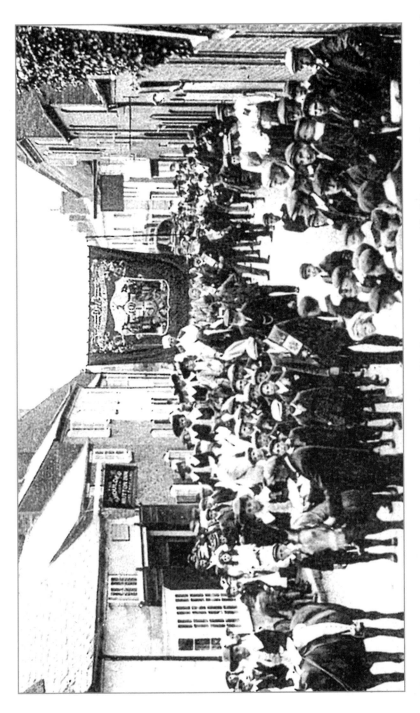

The Ancient Order of Foresters' annual procession in 1908. The Welford Court, known as Welford Rangers, of the organisation was formed on 20th October 1893 by men at the Wheat Sheaf. A detailed account of this friendly society can be found on pages 57 and 58 of *Welford, Portrait of a Northamptonshire Village.*

Foresters' fete 1908. The huge silk banner bore the arms of the order. The organisation in its present form emerged in 1834 from an earlier friendly society the Royal Foresters, which is probably dated from about 1745. In the picture above, standing in the middle in front of the banner is Harry Partridge.

In the saddle ready for the
annual Foresters' parade
are Dick Butlin and Amy
Johnson. The exact year
is unknown.

1951 sees the last march
of the Foresters with
only a handful in the
procession. Norah Johnson
as Maid Marion is
disappearing out of the
picture on a horse.

Coronation parade for George VI 12th May 1937. Top of High Street by Church Lane. Welford had a packed day of activities as the programme on the opposite page shows.

Coronation band of the Foresters takes a breather on the old cricket field.

Contestants in the decorated perambulators and pedal bicycles classes.

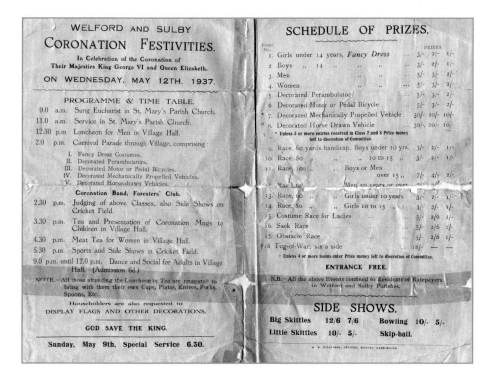

The programme of events for the 1937 Coronation. Note the prizes. Good money for those days.

Fancy dress group in the school playground 1890s.

Daily Mail ball push 1934. This was an annual event on the old cricket field.

George V Jubilee 1935. Dolly Copson and Hilda Keetch span the 25 years.

Every village needs its hall. Above is Welford's as it was in 1906 about a year after completion. In 1929 the hall gained a new entrance and extension as the picture below, from the late 1930s, shows. Mrs. Bowen-Davies paid for the work in memory of her husband.

Tennis courts behind the village hall. The tennis club had the land rent free until the owner, the butcher Mr J. C Martin, reclaimed the site around 1958.

Welford Tennis Club around 1955. Back row from left, Geoff Elson, Bill Gardner and Guy Champion. Front, Eileen Burdham, Norah Johnson, Marjorie Cross. The players on the right are from Market Harborough.

Tennis at Gardner's, 1936. Adults from left, Eric Pettitt, Arthur Pettitt, Frank Gardner, Jessie Gardner, Cyril Pettitt and Jack Haddon. Children, Bill Gardner and Yvonne Pettitt.

Women's Institute 21st Year celebration 1948. The group includes Mrs Paget, Mrs Margaret Chambers (president) and Mrs Bowen-Davies.

W.I. 30th celebration 1957. The line-up includes Ida Twemlow, Mrs Bowen-Davies and Lady Boardman.

One of the
first W.I.
outings in the
1930s was on
a river boat
at Windsor.

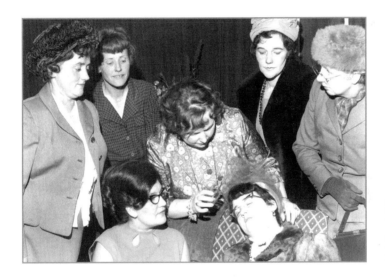

Left and below:
W.I. stage
productions
in the 1960s.

Welford
Brownie pack
in the 1940s.

The Brownies'
21st celebra-
tion party in
the village hall
in May 1950.

The Brownies
presenting
Mrs Bowen-
Davies with a
thank you
badge in the
hall late 1950s.

1930s. Early Welford Amateur Dramatic Society production *Father of the Bride*.

WADS celebrate 21 years in January 1953.

The cast of *Such Things Happen*, a production in October and November 1952. An original programme for the play is shown on the opposite page.

Crucial moment in another WADS production, called *Yellow Sands*.

12

W. A. D. S.

presents

"SUCH THINGS HAPPEN"

on

Thursday, Friday & Saturday

30th, 31st October & 1st November, 1952

P R O G R A M M E

Proceeds for the Welford and Sulby Coronation Fund.

Price 3d.

"SUCH THINGS HAPPEN"

A Comedy - Mystery in Three Acts by Wilfred Massey.

Cast in order of appearance

The entire action of the play takes place in a room in Cliff Edge Cottage, Nurridge - a secluded part on the South East coast of England.

Bertha	Eileen Gilby
"Fishy" Flynn	Peter Walker
David Carter	Robert Cooke
Valerie Morton	Mary Sharp
Philip Manders	David Beeson
Miss Ursula Mannering	Peggy Partridge
Barbara Meadows	Faith Seaton
Herbert Scatters	Jack Gudgeon
Miss Featherstone	Norah Johnson
Detective Inspector Farleigh C.I.D. New Scotland Yard	Fred Seaton

Act I   Scene 1 Morning, Spring
         Scene 2 Afternoon the same day

Act II   Scene 1 Morning of the next day
         Scene 2 A week later. Night.

Act III The Night of the Twenty-third.

Produced by Fred E. Seaton.

Stage Manager Mr. C. Holyland
Scenery by Mr. John Haynes.

Box Office Miss G. Goodfellow
Prompter Miss N. Jenkins

The Society wish to take this opportunity of thanking everyone who has in any way helped with this production.

The first of the WADS' three-act productions, the *Farmer's Wife*, in the 1950s. The photograph on the right was taken outside Rosemary Cottage.

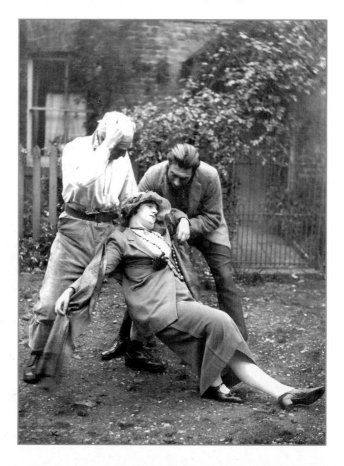

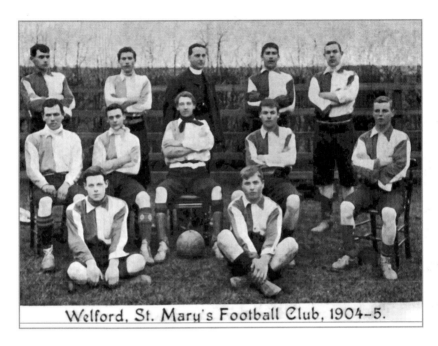

Welford, St. Mary's Football Club, 1904–5.

The earliest photograph of Welford St Mary's Football Club, from 1904–5. Harry Partridge is seated in the centre in front of the vicar.

Welford Victoria in 1908–9. It is not known when the club adopted the name Victoria.

Welford
Victoria in
1947 when
the team was
re-formed.

In 1956 a village meeting
was called and the
team was re-formed,
playing in the Market
Harborough League.

1965. The team had just won the
Harborough Knockout Cup.

Welford cricket team 1946. Back from left, Jack Vaughan, Dick Underwood, Geoff McAlister, Jim Trolly, Stan Graham and Dick Bott. Front, Billy Mann, Herbert Groocock, Bill Illson, Ernie Badger and Cecil Barber. The team disbanded in 1952.

Men's bowls team at the vicarage in the 1930s.

Welford mixed bowls team versus Market Harborough in the 1930s. The bowling green was at the rear of Tyrrell's shop. Albert Tyrrell is tossing the coin.

The carnival procession in 1977, about to leave for a tour of the village.

Queen's Silver Jubilee 1977. From left, Jill Horner, Dolly Fox, Mrs Wattam and Anne Dunn. Photograph taken in front of scout hut.

Launch of the *Welford Bugle* May 1975. Vera and Geoff McAlister on the left with Peggy and Peter Walker. Fellow founder Edwina Redhead is not pictured.

7 Rural Retreats

Sulby Hall 1905. Built in the Palladian style with a large, semi-circular Corinthian columned portico. This early photograph of the hall's glorious setting shows the ornate bridge, which today has been restored for a millennium project.

The south-facing rear of the hall 1905. The gardens were once described as "here no blaze of rare and exotic flora, but rich green lawns such as only England can show, and large beds of antirrhinums – lovable cottage flowers."

Sulby Hall 1914. In 1792 Rene Payne of Welford employed Sir John Soane to design a house on land in the Parish of Sulby. The house, built in 1793–94, was of two storeys with basement and attics. In 1810, Payne's grandson George, 1803–78, inherited the house, and on coming of age in 1824, used the considerable fortune that had accumulated during his minority, to enlarge it. After Major Guy Paget acquired the hall in 1912 a top storey was added to part of the building. The hall was sold in 1952 and demolished, with timbers and other valuable materials being salvaged for use elsewhere.

The Paget coat of arms forms a bridge at the west end of the main lawn in 1917. From 1916 to 1919 Sulby Hall was used as a 50-bed hospital for men wounded in the First World War. They were often seen exercising in this part of the grounds.

Sulby Hall stable block 1950s. This aerial shot shows where at least 20 hunters were kept for riding with the Pytchley hounds. The buildings became Reservoir Farm before being renamed Park Farm in 1952, but they still retain some of the feel of their hunting heyday.

The Pytchley Hunt meets at Sulby Hall in 1913.

Sulby Hall Lodge 1913. Built in 1871 and originally named Blue Cottage, it makes a very stylish entrance for the park. Today it is aptly named Park House.

Staff from Sulby Hall 1912.

The staff in fancy dress at the rear of the hall on New Year's Day 1918. They are watched from the windows by wounded soldiers dressed in hospital 'blues'.

Conservative garden party June 1930. It was held a month before the Pagets left Sulby Hall. A local newspaper reported: "Major Paget said it was a great wrench to leave. The crushing weight of taxation made it impossible for him to keep up the place as it ought to be kept, and he was forced to let it." The Pagets moved to Wheler Lodge on a day when the ill-fated R 101 airship passed overhead.

Mrs Paget opens the recreation ground in the 1950s. Mr Barnes officiates as Mr Martin looks on.

Major and Mrs Paget exercise their Jack Russell in the grounds of Wheler Lodge.

Wheler Lodge in 1907. The house stands back off the Leicester Road north of Welford.

Wheler Lodge around 1947. The house has been enlarged since the picture at the top was taken. A single-storey extension, which today is the kitchen, has been added to the left-hand side. The house was sold for £2,500 in the 1950s after the Pagets left.

The Woolleys, Naseby Road, 1904. George VI, when Duke of York, often stayed here with the Duchess – now the Queen Mother – and their little daughters in the 1930s. In 1938 Princess Elizabeth celebrated her 12th birthday at the Woolleys. She and her sister Margaret visited Gardner's shop in High Street during their visits. Sadly the Woolleys was destroyed by fire in 1947. It was re-built as Naseby Hall.

The Duchess of York and Princess Elizabeth in 1930 or 1931. The exact location is unknown, but the Royal Family often made informal visits to the area from the 1920s to 1970s.

Grange Cottages and stables, Naseby Road 1915. They were built around 1908.

The cottages became the farmhouse for Welford Grange Farm and are pictured here in the 1950s.

A further photograph of the farm in the early to mid 1950s. A giant water tower can be seen between the two haystacks.

The Grange, Naseby Road, Welford 1915. Built around 1908, it was described in 1935 as "a delightfully placed and comfortable residence." The full advertisement from *Field, The Country Newspaper*, is featured on the opposite page. At some time around the 1960s, the section of the house far left, with no downstairs windows and covered in climbing foliage, was demolished, creating a more manageable family residence.

The stables surrounding the courtyard at The Grange 1915. Colonel Faber kept at least 20 horses here. The Prince of Wales, Sir Robert McAlpine and racehorse owner Miss Dorothy Paget were among the distinguished visitors in the 1920s.

THE COUNTRY NEWSPAPER

EDITOR-IN-CHIEF—ERIC PARKER

Telegrams: " *Field Newspaper, London.*"   THE FIELD HOUSE,
Telephone: No. 3682 *Holborn.*   BREAM'S BUILDINGS,
   CHANCERY LANE.

BY AUCTION IN EARLY SUMMER UNLESS SOLD MEANWHILE.

WELFORD GRANGE, NORTHAMPTONSHIRE

THE ABOVE DELIGHTFULLY PLACED AND COMFORTABLE RESIDENCE

contains the following accommodation : Hall, four reception rooms, seven principal bedrooms, day and night nurseries, six secondary bedrooms four bathrooms.

COMPLETE AND
WELL-FITTED OFFICES.
SQUASH COURT.

FIRST-CLASS HUNTING
STABLING.

Set of model dairy farm-buildings for pedigree herd.

SMALLER RESIDENCE.   THREE COTTAGES.

DELIGHTFUL GARDENS AND GROUNDS

Valuable enclosures of pastureland ; area about

50 ACRES

LOW OUTGOINGS AND UPKEEP.

Particulars of JAMES STYLES & WHITLOCK, Rugby.

Saturday, May 4th, 1935

The Manor House from the air late 1950s showing the delightful setting north of St Mary's Church. The gardens extend from West Street to High Street and are completely enclosed by a listed 18th Century wall.

The Manor House was built around 1706 on the site of the old Grange. Indeed, the present house was called the Grange until the 19th Century.

In 1799 John Spencer of the Talbot Inn bought the Manor for a thousand guineas (£1,050). From 1928 to 1942 it was owned by Harry Blundell. Eleanor Campbell then became the owner until 1950 when the house was sold to Lord Boardman.

The Dovecoat was built at the same time as the Manor House in 1706. The sundial is a splendid feature on the south wall.

The Vicarage in Northampton Road 1930. Built in 1810, it was a vicarage until 1977 when it was sold as a private home and renamed Fairfield Lodge.

The Vicarage gardens on a snowy
morning in 1952.

Shrubland House in Northampton Road. Built in the 19th Century, it was once the home of Denys Watkins-Pitchford, the author who wrote and illustrated many nature books as 'BB'.

Interior of Shrubland House, probably in the 1930s or 40s.

The Manse, built in 1799, was one of three almost identical houses erected at that time. The others were The Lodge Farmhouse and Spencer House. The Manse was home to Congregational Church ministers until sold by auction in 1972 and demolished.

Spencer House in West End 1904. Thomas Miller bought it in 1902 with a £1000 loan from a local farmer. The house was sold in 1936 to the Wilson family before being acquired by local milkman Bob Atkinson.

The Doctor's House 1907. Built by John Woodford around 1687, it was occupied by a succession of village doctors, hence the name. It was also named Welford House for a while but should not be confused with the 19th Century house of that name at the southern end of West End. The cricket field was behind the cob wall featured on the opposite side of the road.

Welford House 1907. Built in 1872 by John Wood, it was considerably enlarged between 1908 and 1914. Mrs Bowen-Davies bought it in 1927.

Welford House from the air in the late 1940s. The grounds were set out in the style of garden designer Gertrude Jekyll. Opposite in West End is the timber-framed 17th Century Oak Cottage, which was altered in the 19th Century.

"THE HEMPLOE HILLS" CLUB forms the centre of the Pytchley Hunt and within easy reach of the Fernie Meets, in a beautifully wooded country with an abundance of good Shooting, Fishing, etc. On the west boundary it is joined by the well-known Stanford Park Estate and surrounded by magnificent scenery. It abounds in most beautiful walks and is a splendid resort for a secluded and restful holiday.

From a health standpoint it has the following great advantages:—It is situated 660 feet above the sea level, with a south aspect, a bracing air and water that is celebrated for its purity, thereby making it one of the most charming places in the Midlands.

"THE HEMPLOE HILLS" CLUB has accommodation for a considerable number of Guests. Well-furnished Bedrooms, Spacious Drawing and Dining Rooms, (separate tables), Lounge and Private Sitting Rooms, Baths (hot and cold), Billiards, Bowls, Tennis and Croquet. Excellent Garage. 10 Loose Boxes.

The object of the Proprietor is to provide a Home from Home, combined with good Cuisine, Courtesy and every reasonable attention, at moderate charges. Special terms for week-end visitors.

"THE HEMPLOE HILLS" CLUB is within 4 miles of Welford Station (L. M. & S. Railway). Visitors can be met by Car on receipt of Wire or 'Phone message.

A Dining Room has recently been added to seat 150 persons. Special Catering for Private Parties, Factory Staff Outings, etc. Cricket Ground at the disposal of visitors in fine weather. If wet the Dining Room can be used for Whist Drives, Concerts or Dancing. Estimates given.

Board Residence, £3 3 0 per week
10 6 per day
Bank Holidays £4 4 0
LUNCHEONS & TEAS

Proprietor - A. E. CRANE.
Telegrams : "Crane, Welford 12"
'Phone - - - Welford 12.

From a brochure for the Hemploe Hills Club, probably from the 1930s.

The Hemploe in 1949 with the English Basset Hound puppy show in full swing. Miss Mary Topham laid the foundation stone for this lovely house in August 1863.

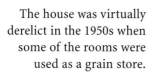

The house was virtually derelict in the 1950s when some of the rooms were used as a grain store.

The Hemploe was destroyed by fire and this is how it looked after being rebuilt in 1974.

In the 1950s The Hemploe became a turkey farm. This is the brochure.

Mr. John Gee, J.P.

Salford House, High Street, 1907. And a rear view. Built in 1882 by John Eyson, it was named after Salford Priors, near Evesham, the Eyson family seat. It was acquired by John Gee JP, left, who was born in 1833. He was the son of George Gee, 1792–1881, known as 'Father' of the Pytchley Hunt, and Mrs Gee, both pictured far left.

The Pytchley Hunt outside Salford House 1907. Before the First World War almost everyone living in the 'big houses' of Welford owned horses and hunted regularly. John Gee had two albums of photographs of famous people who rode with the Pytchley. Five hundred riders were counted in High Street one Boxing Day.

Mrs Bowen-Davies elegantly mounted side-saddle ready for a day's hunting in 1909. There were opportunities for hunting most days from Welford with the Pytchley and Fernie hounds so close.

The Pytchley Hounds in 1909. The Empress of Austria, Earl Spencer, dukes and duchesses were among those who came to the hunt in Welford. The Prince of Wales was a visitor in those days before he became Edward VIII and ultimately Duke of Windsor.

8 The Changing Village

Westfield Crescent, off West Street, was built in 1948 by Brixworth Rural District Council.

The Leys, off Newlands Road, was built in 1970. Prices ranged from around £4,000 for a three-bedroom house to £6,950 for a more spacious one with five bedrooms.

West End 1967. The cob wall to the old cricket field is being demolished ready for the first private estate to be built in Welford. Wakefield Drive, with its 36 homes, is in the making. Prices started at £3,475.

The ground is being cleared.

Building gets under way and...

...the first bungalow nears completion

The sorry-looking former Peacock Inn about to face demolition in 1973.

Most of the building has been reduced to rubble.

And soon the site is cleared ready for the expansion of Wright's haulage business.

The Great Barn, High Street, It was sometimes called Martin's Barn as Mr Martin the butcher kept hens in it. During the Second World War troops were billeted here. In 1962 the barn was bought by Cecil Lane, who reared pigs in it. The building was demolished in 1972 to make way for Salford Close.

Little is known about when the Great Barn was built but today it would surely be a Grade I listed building.

The Great Barn
crumbles as
Salford Close is
about to be built.

1975 and the cottages at the bottom of High Street are about to go. The four stuccoed homes probably date from 1750–60.

The two separate mud-walled cottages were also 18th Century.

Almost gone. And through the gap in the cottages over in West Street the new homes being built on Sulby Rise can be seen.

These cottages, built in 1865, are pictured on 19th April 1974 just a short time before they were demolished. One is the site of the former bakery. The pictures were taken from Sulby Rise.

20th April 1974. The front and
rear of the old cottages which
are about to make way for
two detached houses.

The cottages of 1865 on the bend of West Street still stand. But the gateway seen here
has gone now and the buildings form one home with an annex.

The old barns by Sulby Rise 20th April 1974. The single barn above, housed the old hand-drawn fire cart.

The double barn left, was used as commercial premises.

The Manse House, built in 1799. It was auctioned in 1972 on condition that it was demolished. A sad ending for an elegant home.

Jasmine Cottage around 1900.
It was built in 1736.

Late 1950s. Now called Rosemary Cottage, it has been drastically altered. Some of the timber used in the renovation is thought to have come from Sulby Hall when it was demolished. Sid Hampton and Ted Barber stand outside by an Austin A40.

No 25 High Street. Built in 1954 for Bill and Dorothy Gardner, it was the first private house to be erected in the village since the mid-1920s.

Church Lane as it looked in the 1970s before the new thatched cottages were built. Nos 2 and 4 are Grade II listed buildings.

The old barns in Church Lane early 1970s. Gus Hines kept his cars in the lock-up garages. There used to be a pile of worn-out car parts by the garage door.

Stan Pitcher's former workshop behind No 2 Church Lane. It was demolished when the Elizabethan car park was extended in 1975.

The yard behind No 2 Church Lane. This too was taken for the Elizabethan car park in 1976.

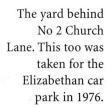

9 Waterways

River Avon 1908. It was called the Greeny Brook locally. Steam lorries stopped at the ford where the crew dropped a hose into the water to recharge their tanks. The men could leave the pump working as they popped across to the George for a drink.

River Avon on a snowy morning in the 1950s. The speed limit signs are in the middle of the bridge, right on the county boundary.

The ford, Welford, 1912. The Avon runs down from the spot where it rises in Naseby to this point by the Naseby turn.

2nd July 1958. Freak flooding at the Naseby turn.

Welford Reservoir late 1950s. The reservoir was used from 1837 to feed the Grand Union canal via the navigable Welford Arm. Sulby Reservoir opened in 1813.

Julia Gilbert by the canal in the 1930s. Born in 1900, she was stricken by polio as a young woman and confined to a wheelchair. She died aged 40.

Welford Lock in 1954.

Michael Brooks and friend by the canal in 1954.

The lock in the late 1940s.

The lift bridge below the lock in the late 1940s. It survived in a dilapidated state until the canal was restored in 1968.

Mary Gilbert of the George Inn on her narrowboat in 1907 with daughters Gwen (with doll) and Julia. The Gwen Mary ferried coal, coke and other essentials up the arm of the Grand Union to the wharf to be delivered by cart to surrounding villages.

The canal in the early 1970s after its restoration.

Along the towpath on a snowy morning in the late 1940s.

The Wharf Inn late 1950s or very early 1960s. The canal is completely neglected. It was another ten years before restoration was completed.

The Wharf June 1970. The restoration was completed in 1969. The opening ceremony in these pictures was attended by Sir Frank Price, Chairman of British Waterways.

10 Welford in Colour

The George Inn 1904. This and the following pictures are from a collection of hand-coloured postcards commissioned by Arthur Goodfellow.

Lower End of High Street around 1920.

High Street by Salford House before 1920.

High Street by Goodfellow's shop and post office 1904.

West End, Welford.

West End. Described by Peter Harrison, a West End resident, as "an unsurpassable view of an English street." Arriving in Welford here you still pass houses "along a corridor of varying warm-coloured red brick, laid in many different bonds, some gauged, some mildly shaded with green lichen, some diaper patterned with 18th Century vitrified flared headers, some hand-made ones and some more modern factory-made."

West End, Welford.

West End by the Chapel and Manse House 1912.

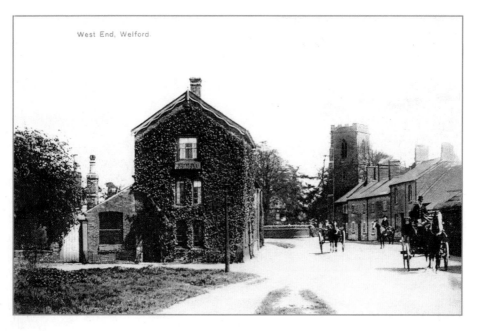

West End by Ivydene 1904.

West Street by the village hall 1912.

West End by Jasmine Cottage 1912. The thatcher is Mr Adnitt.

St Mary's Church 1904.

Naseby Road by the Hollies around 1920.